Scriptures for t

MW00411941

Advent 2009

Celebrate the Newborn Jesus

PAUL E. STROBLE

An Advent Study Based on the Revised Common Lectionary

Abingdon Press / Nashville

CELEBRATE THE NEWBORN JESUS
by Paul E. Stroble

An Advent Study Based on the Revised Common Lectionary

Copyright © 2009 by Abingdon Press

ISBN-13: 978-0-687-65893-0

Manufactured in the United States of America

09 10 11 12 13 14 15 16 17 18—10 9 8 7 6 5 4 3 2 1

ontents

Introduction

Advent is here! The autumn colors have passed, the weather is chillier, and Christmas decorations have adorned businesses for a while. Perhaps your Advent season is like mine: busy. You have the usual tasks and chores, but you also must find time for extra activities such as shopping, cooking, and writing Christmas cards. Church also affords opportunities for worship and service. For instance, I have delivered Angel Tree Christmas gifts for the past several years. December is a month with plenty to do.

The word *advent* is derived from the Latin word *adventus*, which means "coming"; and it names the purpose of this church season. Advent is the time we await Jesus' coming at Bethlehem and his second coming to reign over God's realm. You may know the anxiety of anticipating a baby's birth; however, we do not have to wait for the baby Jesus, thank goodness! Our Advent experience is more symbolic. In waiting for baby Jesus, we open our hearts to the mystery of God becoming human and to the establishment of God's realm of mercy and justice in the fullness of time.

You probably are not making New Year's resolutions yet; but the church year actually begins with the first Sunday of Advent, which in turn is the first of the four Sundays before Christmas. Advent was originally a time of solemnity, repentance, and fasting, similar to Lent. Fasting is no longer a formal aspect of Advent observance, but the purple color of church vestments conveys solemnity according to ancient church traditions. Congregations more than offset that solemnity, though, by decorating with brightly colored trees, garlands, and stars. If we want Advent to be an introspective time of renewal, we have to make the effort.

Spiritual disciplines, worship, prayer, and Bible reading are important during Advent; and they help us remember the good news of the life that Jesus gives. The Bethlehem Baby teaches us that God is present with us in Jesus Christ. Through Christ, God has done everything necessary to accomplish our salvation because we can never earn it, even with the most blameless life. The good news means the power of God's Holy Spirit through Christ is available for us throughout the year. The Advent season teaches us to celebrate these realities and inspires us to spread Christ's love.

Through a series of several Bible passages, we will focus together on "the reason for the season." Let us celebrate the newborn Jesus!

Remembering God's Promises

Scriptures for Advent:
The First Sunday
Jeremiah 33:14-16
1 Thessalonians 3:9-13
Luke 21:25-36

Christmas arrives in about four weeks! What is happening in your life? Are things pretty good or not so good? How is your faith right now? Advent offers the opportunity to hear and reclaim God's promises in Jesus Christ.

It is not always easy to maintain our faith. As Christians, we try to focus upon Jesus throughout the year as we bring our questions, concerns, and petitions before him. Sometimes we drift from God, not always intentionally; but problems distract us, and crises arise that force us to question our assumptions about God. Sometimes happiness and prosperity distract us. It is characteristic of human nature to neglect God when circumstances are less stressful.

However, the gospel of Jesus Christ does not depend on us. God showers us with blessings that we do not earn. God assures us the gift of life through Jesus Christ. Christ breaks the barriers that we raise and helps us grow in love and wisdom. God works through us to spread Christ's love to others.

Traditionally Advent is a time of preparation for Jesus' birth and for his second coming, an aspect of the season that is not always emphasized. In both cases we prepare for and celebrate what God has done and what God continues to do in our world through Jesus Christ.

Our first set of Scriptures help us look again at God's promises and remember that God is always present with us and at work for justice and righteousness. Jeremiah 33:14-16 looks to a time when Israel and Judah will live in the security of God's justice and righteousness. Paul, in 1 Thessalonians 3:9-13, gives assurance about Jesus' blessings as he writes to Christians struggling in their faith. In Luke 21:25-36, Jesus speaks with hope concerning difficult times as signs of redemption and the coming of the Son of Man.

As nostalgic as this season can be, Advent is not just about looking back to Jesus' birth long ago. Advent is also about Jesus' life now and his promises for all the future.

A SECURE, RIGHTEOUS FUTURE
JEREMIAH 33:14-16

Have you ever gotten good news when you most needed it? At a time when I was discouraged about my employment, God opened up an amazing job opportunity. I also remember getting a clean bill of health after an extended time of uncertainty about a medical diagnosis. Good news at such times is wonderful; but when no good news comes, we must endure our difficult circumstance to its conclusion. I have been in those situations; and I have learned that hard times can offer opportunities to seek God's help, to deepen one's spiritual life, and to experience God's care.

If we have distress in our lives, we can use this season as a time for hope. My family and I usually put the Christmas tree up in early December; but one year, I put up the tree on Veteran's Day just because I needed some extra cheer and hope! My best friend in college struggled with cancer for years and used Christmas as a hopeful milestone. He lost the struggle with cancer; but while he was alive, Christmas helped him focus on Christ and all God's promises.

The Jeremiah passage is a classic statement of hope: "The days are surely coming, says the LORD, when I will fulfill the promise I made to the house of Israel and the house of Judah" (Jeremiah 33:14). This announcement is particularly wonderful because of the terrible circumstances in which Jeremiah spoke. At that moment, the Babylonians were on the verge of conquering Jerusalem; and the king had confined Jeremiah in the court of the guard (32:2-3).

From the time of the judges until the fall of Jerusalem to the Babylonians, the people struggled with issues of faithfulness and fidelity to God's covenant. After Solomon's reign, the kingdom that was united by David was divided into two different kingdoms––Israel in the north and Judah in the south (922 B.C.). During the succession of kings that followed David and Solomon, the prophets preached against the people's participation in pagan religions, their neglect of issues of justice, and their forgetfulness of God. Israel fell to the Assyrians in 722 B.C. Judah was taken over by Babylonia from 597 to 587 B.C. Jerusalem fell, and its leading citizens were exiled in Babylonia in 587 B.C.

Jeremiah was a prophet at a dark time in Judah's history. He lived about 600 years before Jesus, beginning his prophetic ministry during the final years of King Josiah's reign, around the year 626 B.C. and continuing after the fall of Jerusalem. In his preaching, Jeremiah pronounced God's judgments upon Judah's most sacred institutions: the Davidic monarchy, Jerusalem, and the Temple. He dared to compare Jerusalem to Shiloh, the Israelites' first sanctuary, which was apparently destroyed by the Philistines (1 Samuel 4:10-12; Jeremiah 26:1-9). However, to Jeremiah's contemporaries, the sacredness of Jerusalem and the Temple was a point of straightforward faith in God's goodness. They reacted to his warnings with anger and rejection.

The last king of Judah tried to ward off the Babylonian threat. He maintained peace for 11 years, but eventually the Babylonians lay siege on Jerusalem and took the city in 587 (2 Kings 24:18-25; Jeremiah 52:30). As a result, the people of Judah spent long years in exile.

What a terrible tragedy for God's people! They experienced the loss of everything dear to them. However, Jeremiah, as God's prophet, helped the people look into the future to a better time not only when security and peace returned but when the kingdom would be just and equitable for all. In spite of dire circumstances and imminent loss, Jeremiah told the people that the best times were ahead. What is the promise of Jeremiah 33:14? The Lord promised a king to rule his people (2 Samuel 7:4-17), a "branch" from the lineage of David who would rule wisely and with strength. The people would be secure and would enjoy justice and righteousness.

Describing the coming days, the prophet uses the word *righteous* three times: the righteous branch of David, the righteousness in the land, and the righteousness of the Lord. We tend to think of righteousness as moral character. The Hebrew word also means "justice," "rightness," "prosperity," "salvation," and "moderation." In the land described in Jeremiah 33, the new Davidic king will rule according to God's will: Those in need will be provided for, people will care for their neighbor, people will live rightly, and the people will love God and neighbor alike according to the commandments (Leviticus 19:18; Deuteronomy 6:5).

While turmoil continues in our world and in our lives, so does God's vision for justice and righteousness. Jeremiah proclaimed the promise of a Davidic king who would bring justice and righteousness to the land. Christians see this promise fulfilled in Jesus Christ and, as his followers, choose to live as just and righteous people. Christians understand Jesus as the confirmation of Jeremiah's words of hope and promise. As we read this passage with Jesus in mind, we see how Jeremiah's prophecies of a great king were fulfilled in the Baby born in David's city (Luke 2:10-11). We see how the new covenant predicted earlier in Jeremiah 31:31 is fulfilled in the body and blood of Jesus shed for us (Luke 22:19-20).

You may ask, not inappropriately, why all the prophecies have not yet come true. We sing "peace on earth" during this holiday season, and yet we do not see it. We long for peace, justice, and righteousness to be found in our world. Our own lives become filled with turmoil, and we cry out for help. Perhaps Jeremiah's greatest insight is that God's very nature is justice and righteousness. "The LORD is our righteousness." Our future and our ultimate security rest here. No matter what is going on in our lives, Jeremiah's words offer the hope of God's presence, a presence that promises ultimate justice and righteousness for all creation.

When did you face a time of loss of a dream and discover that God was at work to sustain you or to provide something brand new in your life? What does it mean to you to understand God's nature as just and righteous?

STEADFAST IN FAITH
1 THESSALONIANS 3:9-13

My wife and I have lived in several towns around the country. We send nearly 150 Christmas cards each year, which is one of my upcoming Advent tasks. (I have this down to a science.) Beth and I enjoy keeping in touch with friends over the long haul.

One cannot always explain the reasons for rapport between people. Sometimes shared experiences and similar points of view create friendships, but not always. In my line of work, I have known people that I like; but when we are together, we do not have much to say. On the other hand, I have close friends who have different interests than mine. My mother has a friendship that began in the early 1930's when she and her friend walked to a one-room schoolhouse. They have always had completely opposite political views, but they have never let the different views affect their relationship.

First Thessalonians 3:9-13 is a wonderful expression of friendship. Scholars believe Thessalonians may be the earliest of Paul's several epistles. Paul, Silvanus, and Timothy had founded the Thessalonian church (Acts 17:1-8). As Paul traveled, he heard of troubles at the church. Of course, he had none of the instant communication that we enjoy; he had to wait to get news. He planned to return to the church, but he told them "Satan blocked [their] way" (1 Thessalonians 2:18). Timothy brought Paul favorable news about the church, much to Paul's relief; and his letter to them expresses love and affirmation.

What was wrong at Thessalonica? The Jewish Christians at the church experienced pressure from those who still practiced traditional Jewish worship, but the church also contained Gentile converts who had not been raised in the high moral standards of traditional Judaism. This mix of people, in turn, suffered from the treatment of non-Christians toward their fellowship. Thus, Paul worried that the church people might abandon their faith under pressure.

We do not usually suffer the hostile persecution to which the Bible alludes. Saint Teresa of Avila, Spanish Carmelite, wrote, "It is amusing to see souls who, while they are at prayer, fancy they are willing to be despised and publicly insulted for the love of God, yet afterwards do all they can to hide their small defects; if anyone unjustly accuses them of a fault, God deliver us from their outcries!"[1]

The Thessalonians suffered actual persecution, not just hurt feelings. What if you were under pressure because of your faith for a prolonged period? Paul was overjoyed that the Christians remained steadfast. He even put them in the same league as the church in Judea where Christianity began (2:14).

Paul had other concerns with the church: Some of the people were busybodies (4:11), some did not like Paul (hinted at in 2:5-10), and others worried that those who had died would miss Christ's blessings (4:13-18). Paul and his church looked to the quick return of Jesus, which added urgency to his letter. Not only did Paul worry about them, but he also wanted them to be faithful so they would be ready for the return of Jesus.

In 1 Thessalonians 3:9-13, Paul reminds the people to continue in faith: "May the Lord make you increase and abound in love for one another and for all, just as we abound in love for you. And may he so strengthen your hearts in holiness that you may be blameless before our God and Father at the coming of our Lord Jesus with all his saints" (verses 12-13). The Thessalonian church already knew how to love one another, and they showed love to others (4:9-10). However, even though loving feelings may last a long time, godly love may require vigilance and faithfulness lest it slip away amid church tensions, personal troubles, and turmoil. God's love includes forgiveness, service, mercy, compassion, justice, fellowship—all of which focus on mutual well-being. In essence and spirit, Paul called them to remember who they were and to whom they belonged.

What makes a congregation "click"? If you have been a member of several churches, you may have felt that you never quite fit in with one congregation, while in another congregation you remember experiencing a wonderful fellowship. A pastor might have a lovely, warm partnership with the people of one church; but another congregation might treat the same pastor with criticism and resistance. One congregation might be filled with people eager to serve, while another might have comparatively few local ministries and many problems.

I find heartening the fact that Paul had similar experiences. He dealt with all kinds of problems in letters to the churches. Paul's letter to the Galatians, for instance, addresses the larger issue of whether Gentiles had to convert to Judaism and practice the Law in order to be Christians. His letters to the church at Corinth address conflict over such issues as food sacrificed to idols, the Lord's Supper, devotion to wisdom, spiritual gifts, and the collection that would fund Paul's travels. Paul's letters contain advice about gossiping, fault-finding, and the importance of affirming and supporting one another.

Paul tended to wear his heart on his sleeve when he wrote to the churches, a quality that I find encouraging. We esteem toughness and directness in people, but those traits often mask that person's true qualities. Although Paul used rhetorical devices of persuasion and self-presentation common in the letter writing of the time, you get the sense of genuineness and authenticity in his feelings toward his congregations. Paul was relieved when he learned that his friends in Thessalonica had remained steadfast in their faith. He prayed for their continued growth in love so that they would be prepared for the coming of Jesus.

It is sometimes challenging to remember how to encourage one another in love in relationships that are strained. We all know someone who we consider to be irritating or difficult. It requires special effort to be civil to such persons. On some level, however, we realize that love and warm emotions are not always the same thing. Holy love that comes from God involves acting for the good of another. When we remember that God strengthens our capacity to love one another, we can find ways to relate that are not harmful and that will contribute to the good of the community as a whole.

What are some ways you, as an individual Christian, can strengthen your capacity to "abound in love" for those around you? What actions would express God's love toward those you find hard to love?

A CERTAIN HOPE
LUKE 21:25-36

I have a strange memory from junior high school, about 1970. Those were crazy times to start with; but at our school, a rumor spread that a baby had been born somewhere and had miraculously announced that the world would end in 24 hours. According to the rumor, everyone in the delivery room promptly died! I do not know where this silly, creepy story came from. How, you may ask, did the news spread if everyone in the story died? However, several of my classmates got spooked. Girls were crying in the bathroom. One of my teachers stopped class and talked to the students about the power of rumors.

I thought of that incident when I read Luke 21:26: "People will faint from fear and foreboding of what is coming upon the world." A rumor can cause anxiety, but "fear and foreboding" can happen over more dire circumstances. I remember the horror that followed the assassinations in the 1960's. My parents recalled the tense years prior to and during America's entry into World War II. My grandmother remembered with abiding chill the horrors of World War I. None of us, of course, can forget September 11 and the difficulties of the ensuing years as our nation considered responses to terrorism.

I said earlier that Advent traditionally honors not only Jesus' first coming at Bethlehem but also his second coming. In fact, the New Testament refers several times to the coming of Jesus (Matthew 24:27; 1 Thessalonians 3:13; 4:15; 2 Peter 3:4; and 1 John 2:28). The Greek word is *parousia*; and its meaning carries the ideas of arrival, presence, and the destruction of wickedness. Even though centuries separate Jesus' first coming from his promised return, many Christians have found great comfort in the hope of his return, his presence, and the restoration of God's realm of justice and mercy.

It may feel strange to think about the end of time when we are celebrating Christmas. However,

our focus is not on the end of time as an isolated subject; our focus is on Jesus. The Jesus who is born at Bethlehem is the same Jesus who died for our sins and rose again. Mary's Baby is the same Jesus who frees us from the anxiety that we must earn our salvation. The promise of his return and presence reminds us that life has meaning and purpose amid even the worst circumstances.

Luke 21:5-36 contains Jesus' teachings about the coming of God's realm. In verses 5-24, Jesus warns about the destruction of the Temple (verses 5-6), the eventual imprisonment and persecution of the disciples, and the destruction of Jerusalem. Immediately following this section with its description of destruction, verses 25-36 offer signs of hope on a cosmic scale.

Jesus talked about the coming of the Son of Man, a messianic figure used by Jesus in reference to himself. In the midst of terror and destruction, Jesus told the disciples they would see " 'the Son of Man coming in a cloud' with power and great glory" (verse 27). The images of the shaken heavens and the heavenly bodies (verses 25-26) echo the words and ideas of the prophets in Isaiah 13:10; Joel 2:10; 3:3-4; and Zephaniah 1:15. Jesus told the disciples that when such signs occur, "stand up and raise your heads, because your redemption is drawing near" (Luke 21:28). He continued with the lesson of the fig tree in order to emphasize the hope of a better day. Jesus' vision of God's future offered hope that would carry them through times of destruction and persecution.

Jesus' words to the disciples offer hope and help us as we look to the future during difficult times. Respecting the uncertainties of the future is a good thing. All of us have better hindsight than foresight; but we can prepare for potential emergencies. We can try to anticipate problems and head them off. All the while, we place our trust in God because the ultimate control of our future is in God's hands, not ours.

We all know we will die someday. Mozart once said, "I never lie down at night without reflecting that—young as I am—I may not live to see another day. Yet no one of all my acquaintances could say that in company I am morose and disgruntled. For this blessing I daily thank my Creator and wish with all my heart that each one of my fellow-creatures could enjoy it."[2]

Sometimes we enjoy the blessing of a day of life because of personal circumstances. My grandmother died in her sleep in a house fire when I was 15. That event gave me a lifelong lesson that no one knows what is ahead in life. Consequently, I have tried to live my life mindful of being as positive an influence for others as possible. Jesus helps us trust that God uses our lives for good.

Jesus' teachings also prevent us from becoming lax. Not long after September 11, we groaned at the long lines and heightened security in airports. Now, airport security is anticipated and accepted. Bible scholar William Barclay notes that we should be people "in a permanent sate of expectation."[3] Rather than living in a state of neglectful autopilot, we can hope for the fullness of Christ's presence. We can feel happy and hopeful at God's steadfast love.

We can live hopefully because God's promises are absolutely certain. I believe God works constantly to remind us of that. I also believe that God prepares us to be ready. Thus the power of Jesus' words: We should not succumb to "the worries of this life" in case the day of the Lord should "catch you unexpectedly, like a trap" (verses 34-35). We can take heart in Jesus' promise that "the kingdom of God is near" (verse 31) and that Jesus' words "will not pass away" (verse 33), no matter what is happening in our lives and in our world.

If you knew how much longer you had to live, what would you do? How can your alertness to the promise of God's coming kingdom invigorate your life of faith?

---

[1] From *Ordinary Graces: Christian Teachings on the Interior Life,* edited by Lorraine Kisley (Bell Tower, 2000); page 38.
[2] From *Mozart: Traces of Transcendence,* by Hans Kung (William B. Eerdmans Publishing Company, 1991); page 24.
[3] From *The Gospel of Luke,* by William Barclay in The Daily Bible Studies Series (The Westminster Press, 1975); page 261.

Opening Our Hearts to God's Promises

Scriptures for Advent:
The Second Sunday
Malachi 3:1-4
Philippians 1:3-11
Luke 3:1-6

As a kid, I thought of Thanksgiving as an informal beginning point for the Christmas season. Around the time of the big family meal, I started to focus my attention on the bountiful blessings of the Sears holiday catalog, not for things to order but for things to request from Santa.

However, my childhood Christmases were not totally materialistic. My mother made sure I had a good church background. I participated in Christmas pageants, learned religious carols, and memorized a few basic holiday Scriptures. I loved the big, colorful, extravagant aspects of Christmas; but I gained a good sense of the true meaning of Christmas.

As adults, many of us continue to balance the sacred and secular aspects of Christmas. Lots of things, including possessions, vie for our attention. We experience difficult demands at work; but over time we realize that because of various pressures we have changed over time. We have become different people, perhaps people we did not want to be; and we are not sure what to do. Sometimes we realize that our faith has not sufficed for changed circumstances; but all the while, God has been working in our lives in order to help us see our true meaning and purpose.

During these weeks of Advent, we prepare for the coming of the baby Jesus in Bethlehem. However, Jesus has already been born, so for what are we preparing? We focus on Jesus and deepen our trust in God's promises. We open our hearts to the work God may be beginning and continuing in our lives. We think about the ways God has already prepared and promised salvation to people through the ages.

Our Scripture passages this Sunday concern the blessings of God's work within us. Malachi 3:1-4 predicts the time when God's messenger would announce the coming of the Lord. Paul reminds the church at Philippi in Philippians

1:3-11 to grow in knowledge and love that produces a harvest of righteousness. Luke 3:1-6 tells of the appearance of God's messenger John the Baptist.

These passages call us to consider what work God is beginning and continuing in our lives. They offer an opportunity to reflect on opening our hearts to God's promises in our daily lives of faith.

LIKE A
REFINER'S FIRE
MALACHI 3:1-4

My wife's first husband (who was also my best friend in college) died when he was 29. Beth and I married in Illinois, lived for a time in Virginia, and then moved to Arizona. While in Arizona, Beth decided to take her previous wedding ring to a local jeweler and have it refashioned into a new ring, which she still wears. Not only the gold but the memories it carries are precious to both of us.

Years ago, I underlined 1 Peter 1:6-7 in my Bible: "Even if now for a little while you have had to suffer various trials, so that the genuineness of your faith—being more precious than gold that, though perishable, is tested by fire—may be found to result in praise and glory and honor when Jesus Christ is revealed." I liked the image of gold being used to represent faith as precious to God. I also liked that verse because it offered hope whenever trouble happened.

I connect that verse with Malachi 3:1-4, which talks about the fire and refinement of God. Verses 1-3 were set to music by Handel in his oratorio *Messiah* (Part 1, numbers 5-7). The soloist requires amazing vocal control for the phrase "refiner's fire." The musical line sounds like the restlessness of flames.

Malachi is the last book in the Old Testament. Scholars date the book from the post-exilic period (after 539 B.C., more specifically during the mid-400's B.C.), the time when the people of Judah returned from Babylonian exile, rebuilt Jerusalem and the Temple, and restored national and religious life. The book refers to Temple sacrifices, the tithe, foreign wives, and other issues contemporary to the time period.

We do not know much about Malachi himself. In fact, scholars have wondered whether that was his name, because the word *malachi* also means "my messenger," a phrase used in verse 1. Malachi looked to his own time and to a future time when the Day of the Lord arrives.

Verses 1-4 connect back to 2:17, where God warns that the people have "wearied" the Lord with their questions and conclusions about God's justice. Malachi's style is logical. God sounds like a debater in this book's distinctive statement-question-answer format. Questions about God's justice are not only appropriate, they occur in other Scriptures as well. The Psalms contain many prayers questioning God's slowness to vindicate the people.

Books such as Habakkuk and Job, also raise questions about God's justice. As Holy Scripture, these writings ask sincere questions about God's purposes. In the context of Malachi, however, the people had broken the covenant (Malachi 1:6-7; 2:8-9, 14-16; 3:8-9, 13-14); and rather than being introspective and repentant, they directed questions back to God. The people said, "All who do evil are good in the sight of the LORD, and he delights in them. . . . Where is the God of justice?" (2:17).

Later, God addressed these concerns (3:5, 13–4:3). God promised to return to his Temple and bring justice; but look out! "Who can endure the day of his coming, and who can stand when he appears?" (3:2). I once heard a preacher say that we should be careful when we ask God to correct the wicked because none of us are righteous. All of us are guilty of creating and perpetuating injustice and going against God's holy will. When the day of God's coming arrives, no one is immune from the fire of God's presence and righteousness.

God's presence is elsewhere depicted in terms of fire: the burning bush (Exodus 3:2), the death of Aaron's sons (Leviticus 10:1-3), the Lord's presence on Sinai (Deuteronomy 4:11), and the miraculous sacrifice offered by Elijah (1 Kings 18:30-40). In the New Testament, too, the judgment of God appears as a fire (Hebrews 10:27). By mentioning offerings (Malachi 3:3-4), Malachi also alludes to the fire of God's sacrificial altar where the Levitical priests offered sacrifices on behalf of the people.

Malachi uses two different images of refinement. The first is the image of fire that purifies gold and silver. Gold and silver are precious for their rarity, beauty, and malleability. Gold is durable and does not oxidize. When gold is heated, it melts and becomes better as the impurities are burned off. Both metals have the additional quality of being reflective. The second is the image of the preparation of newly woven cloth. A fuller was a person who prepared new cloth, and fullers' soap was a strong alkali that cleansed the cloth.

These double-edged metaphors seem harsh. Who wants to think about spiritual growth as being burned or scrubbed with a strong alkali? Who enjoys recalling circumstances that could be described as "passing through fire"? On the other hand, imagine God considering you as something precious, such as fine, new cloth or, even better, as gold and silver.

The idea of tough times as God's will or as God's way of purifying or refining us presents challenges. Hebrews 12:7-11 says that God disciplines those he loves. In Matthew 5:45, Jesus teaches that pain and suffering come to people regardless of their goodness or wickedness.

It can be devastating to think of trouble as being "God's will"; but while we do not attribute every trouble to God, we can affirm that trouble provides an opportunity to draw closer to God. Trouble has many sources, and we all go through a certain refinement in the process of living. Successes, failure, good times, painful events, and abandoned dreams all contribute to who we are.

In all of life, God remains with us as a loving parent who cares for us. God uses all kinds of circumstances for good in order that we become the people God wants us to be. When we open our hearts to God's refining fires, we can discover the blessing of becoming more the person that God knows us to be. In such times we can also discover the blessing of God's love and support.

What times in your life were refining? How did you experience God's presence and care during those times?

HARVEST OF RIGHTEOUSNESS PHILIPPIANS 1:3-11

Do you have people in your life who are there for you? I can name people in my life who are there for me when I am in distress. For instance, a few years ago I felt blue on the anniversary of my father's death, so I called on my friends, spent time with them, and got their advice. Close friendships and nurturing attitudes of others in our lives are key components in our continuing growth as Christians. If you have such people in your life, you understand Paul's feelings when he wrote, "I thank my God every time I remember you, constantly praying with joy in every one of my prayers for all of you. . . . It is right for me to think this way about all of you, because you hold me in your heart. . . . For God is my witness, how I long for all of you with the compassion of Christ Jesus" (Philippians 1:3-4, 7-8). Paul's letter to the Philippians demonstrates a generous, personal affection and a close relationship with the church.

Paul had a vision that he could visit Macedonia and preach (Acts 16:9-10). Then he visited Philippi, a large Macedonian city. Although he and Silas were imprisoned there, they had the occasion to meet Lydia the cloth dealer and were able to begin a group of Christians (Acts 16:11-40). Later, Paul and his friends visited Philippi again (Acts 20:1-6). All the biblical references demonstrate that the Philippians and Paul were there for one another (Philippians 4:15-16).

Paul wrote his letter from prison, perhaps in Rome or Ephesus. When I think about prison as the setting for Paul's letters, I remember the times I have visited prisons. I have taught classes for prison inmates, and I have felt the frightening sensation of doors being closed and locked as I entered the facility. I hate feeling trapped, as I felt in a long shopping line recently; but my "traps" are innocuous. Paul's experience seems unlike mine. He was astonishingly upbeat in this letter. In fact, he rejoiced later that his incarceration had helped him spread the gospel among the guards and prison population and also had empowered others to share the gospel more boldly (Philippians 1:12-14).

Being a Christian is not always an upbeat, victory-to-victory process. As we saw in Malachi, God's refinement can be difficult, depending on what within us needs to be refined. Sometimes we hate to admit to other Christians that our faith is imperfect. Prayer is a struggle, witnessing does not come easily, and church does not "speak" to us. We hate to admit that we are out of kilter for fear other Christians will disapprove. Take heart!

Our passage tells us that God begins a good work in our hearts and lives and brings it to completion. That good work includes the maturing of our knowledge and righteousness and the transformative power of God's love. Although we may put ourselves in position to receive God's blessings, God continually works within us to help us transform into holy Christians and, according to Paul, to produce a "harvest of righteousness" (verse 11).

Do you consider yourself to be righteous? If you think righteousness has to do with exemplary moral achievement, pure motives, extraordinary sacrifice, and a high level of selfless love, you probably think, *Yeah, right.* Righteousness, though, as translated from the original Greek, has to do with equity and justice "that comes through Jesus Christ for the glory and praise of God" (verse 11). It carries the sense of gaining God's righteousness, that is, God's just and equitable nature, through our relationship with Jesus Christ, then seeing righteousness grow within us so that we "may be pure and blameless" (verse 10).

In my hometown, I am usually connected with other people: my parents and grandparents, my cousins who run a downtown store, and a popular local family with the same surname as mine. Family associations provide a sense of belonging and identity. Righteousness works similarly in that whether or not we are stereotypically good people, we are righteous because we belong to God. We share the righteousness of God through Jesus Christ.

God also transforms us. Paul did not refer to Christian virtues but rather to fruit of the Spirit: kindness, love, peace, joy, patience, generosity, self-control, gentleness, and faithfulness (Galatians 5:22-23). Consider the Holy Spirit as the living tree and the Spirit's "produce" as the characteristics of God that are evidenced in your life. Paul used similar agricultural language: "This is my prayer, that your love may overflow more and more with knowledge and full insight to help you to determine what is best, so that in the day of Christ you may be pure and blameless, having produced the harvest of righteousness that comes through Jesus Christ for the glory and praise of God" (Philippians 1:9-11).

As Christians, we often fall into the trap of believing that our righteousness is the result of our own efforts. Notice that Paul put the initiative and power on God rather than on us. He prayed that the Philippians "may be pure and blameless, having produced the harvest of righteousness *that comes through Jesus Christ* for the glory and praise of God" (verses 10-11, emphasis added).

We, too, need to affirm that the real work is God's rather than ours. Plenty of people have good moral character, and that is quite important. However, if we focus solely on personal character, we are liable to miss the emphasis on God's free grace and power. You can be a highly imperfect, struggling person whose life is a total mess; and you may be closer to God than upright Christians who think their righteousness is due to their good deeds.

At the same time that we recognize God's free gift of grace, we open our hearts to ways we can participate with God and let God's work of grace find fruition in our actions. Out of our gratitude and recognition of God's active work within us, we choose to act with God's purposes in our lives and relationships.

By definition, righteousness is communal. Our relationship with God through Jesus Christ nurtures the growth of love for God and love for others. Such love manifests in righteous fruit or harvest—acts of service, mercy, justice, and love through which we glorify God. God's love and grace are the source and the harvest of our righteousness.

Who are the people in your life who are there for you? Who nurtures you as you grow in love of God and neighbor? How do you see the harvest of righteousness in your life?

PREPARE THE WAY
LUKE 3:1-6

Have you ever met someone who is famous? When I was five, I met president Harry S. Truman and shook his hand. I said hello to actor Jody Foster once. We attended the same university in the early 1980's. One evening, she was in line behind me at the campus pizza parlor.

The faces and lives of celebrities and other well-known figures are on display in the media, and their lives influence the culture in positive and negative ways. I am amused when I read about the life lessons these public figures have learned. Do we equate fame and wisdom? On a human level, I am glad when celebrities deal with their lives in a positive way; but I dislike the implied notion that celebrities are authoritative sources of life lessons or that they "prepare the way" for us to live a meaningful life.

John the Baptist was an influential person in his own way. He was not a nobody. He was the son of Zechariah, who belonged to a priestly order, and Elizabeth, who was a descendant of Aaron (Luke 1:5). His birth recalls other births to previously barren women such as the births of Jacob and Esau, sons of Rebekah and Isaac (Genesis 25:21); and Samuel, son of Hannah and Elkanah (1 Samuel 1:20). For those who recognized God's work, John's prophetic call was momentous, for no prophet had appeared among the Jews for over 400 years.

Luke gives information about the circumstances of John's birth and then introduces him dramatically in Chapter 3. Luke dates the beginning of John's prophetic ministry from "the fifteenth year of the reign of Emperor Tiberius, when Pontius Pilate was governor of Judea" (Luke 3:1). The description continues through several Roman and Jewish rulers. I think of certain movies where a scene begins with a wide shot of landscape and moves in toward a specific thing or a specific person. Luke's point is subtle but noticeable: All these influential people lived at the time John the Baptist preached. John was the focus of God's great work in the lives of his people.

Over 25 years ago, I visited Israel and Jordan. I enjoyed visiting the area of the Jordan River and the Dead Sea. The landscape around the salty Dead Sea is barren. Further north, the river area has more vegetation and is much more inviting. The traditional site of Jesus' baptism is in this area, and it was here that John the Baptist attracted crowds with his prophetic preaching.

Much of verses 1-6 is a quotation, slightly modified, from Isaiah 40:3-5. In biblical times, the expression "prepare the way of the Lord" (Luke 3:4) alluded to the travels of a monarch or other important leader. Back then, roads followed uneven terrain; and all kinds of hazards, natural and human, might meet a traveler. As the king approached, a royal entourage might clear the roads and attempt to find the best way.

The image has a contemporary resonance for me. My father was a truck driver. The history and character of highways interests me. In the early days of American automobile travel, roads were dirt or gravel. The first highways simply followed existing roads no matter how many curves and right-angle turns. A major 1910's transcontinental highway, for instance, made five right-angle turns as it passed through my hometown. Today's interstate highways do not even pass through small towns; they proceed straight through the countryside.

Isaiah uses highway imagery to refer to the return from exile in Babylon in which God's glory and victory would appear in the journey through the wilderness. The paths will be cleared; all the crooked, rough roads will become straight and smooth; and the valleys will be filled in. John connects with the ancient message of Isaiah in order to point again, in his time, to the revelation of God's glory. His pronouncement sets the stage for "all flesh" to "see the salvation of God" (verse 6).

The expression "It's amazing what can get done when no one cares who gets credit" is not practical if you are in a job where your work performance is scrutinized. However, the expression points to a truth: When we work together and support and affirm one another in our respective roles,

great things can happen. I thought of that when I recalled a painting of the Crucifixion by Matthias Grünewald. John the Baptist anachronistically stands to the side and points to a particularly tragic and gruesome Christ. That was John's fame and great task. He pointed to Jesus so people could find their way to the Savior.

As we open our hearts to God's promises, we too can point to Jesus. We are more fully ourselves when we work together to point beyond ourselves to the fulfillment of God's promises in Jesus Christ. In so doing, we prepare the way, as individuals and as a community of faith, for God's active work in our midst.

How have you experienced God's presence in the wilderness places of your life? As you look back to this time, how was the road made straight; and how were the rough places made smooth?

Finding Hope in God's Promises

Scriptures for Advent:
The Third Sunday
Zephaniah 3:14-20
Philippians 4:4-7
Luke 3:7-18

A few years ago, I wrote a study book about different religions of the world. I interviewed people about their beliefs so that the study book would contain real explanations by religious worshipers themselves and not simply my interpretations. Something that struck me was the ease with which some of my interviewees spoke about their beliefs.

One man talked articulately for over half an hour about his faith, without prior preparation. I wondered how well some of us could do that. Could we explain to a person unacquainted with Christianity who Jesus is, why he died, what the Resurrection means, the difference between faith and works, the responsibilities with which God entrusts us, and the blessings God provides for us? Do we actually live our lives within the hope of God's promises?

If we think we could not explain Christianity to someone, maybe our faith is so personal that we have trouble putting it into words; or maybe we feel shy doing so because we are self-conscious. Maybe we do not fully understand what we believe. Maybe we do not fully comprehend the hope God offers us through Jesus Christ. Many of us attend church our whole lives but do not grasp the fullness of the gospel message. We hold on to the idea that being a Christian is about "being a good person" rather than being saved and empowered by God's Spirit through Jesus Christ. We can, however, experience a deep, abiding hope as we reclaim God's promises and live our lives based on the hope of God's promises.

Advent can be a good time to assess our faith and a positive way to start a new church year. We can reflect on the things that make us happy and consider whether our Christian faith gives us a comparable happiness. We can think about whether we live in the hope of God's promises. If not, what might be the reasons? If our faith does give us hope, what are those reasons? Could we share with other people why our faith is important? Could we share our hope with others?

This week's study offers hope that consequently becomes a reason for great joy. Zephaniah 3:14-20 proclaims the promise of God's presence and restoration of Israel as a reason for songs and shouts. Philippians 4:4-7 calls for rejoicing in the Lord. In Luke 3:7-18, a passionate John the Baptizer proclaims that the Messiah, God's anointed, will come to baptize with the Holy Spirit. These Scriptures inspire us to take time this season to find hope in our faith as we reclaim God's promises.

SING AND SHOUT!
ZEPHANIAH 3:14-20

One of my favorite movies is *American Splendor,* about the Cleveland comic book writer Harvey Pekar. Harvey is treated for cancer. Later, Harvey is talking on the phone while his wife, Joyce, is working on a project. When he hangs up, he tells his wife, "That was the doctor." Harvey is glum, but the character is always glum, so you do not know what the outcome will be. Joyce looks at him expectantly. "He says I'm all clear." Of course, palpable relief fills the room.

Many of us know the feeling of such relief. We have experienced trouble or illness that eventually

came to an end. We know how it feels to get the "all clear" message, perhaps in a letter about the situation or in a call from the doctor. When that good news comes, what a relief! Once again, we experience hope instead of worry about an outcome.

Our Scripture reading in Zephaniah offers hope and a reason to sing and shout even though the good news is given to a "soiled, defiled, oppressing city" that "has accepted no correction. . . . Not trusted the LORD . . . not drawn near to God"(Zephaniah 3:1-2). The condition of the people makes God's promises all the more remarkable.

Zephaniah ben Cushi is one of the Minor Prophets, which means the Book of Zephaniah is shorter in length compared to those of the Major Prophets Isaiah, Jeremiah, and Ezekiel. Zephaniah was not only a prophet, but may have been a member of the royal family. His great-great-grandfather was Hezekiah (Zephaniah 1:1) and may have been the king who reigned in Judah in about 715–687 B.C. Zephaniah prophesied during the 600's B.C. at a slightly earlier time period than Jeremiah, prior to the Babylonian destruction of Jerusalem. Zephaniah 1:14-18 describes the "great day of the LORD" in terms full of judgment and doom.

Jerusalem was condemned for its wickedness (3:1-5); but divine judgment is not limited to the people of Judah, for in Chapters 2 and 3, we also find words of warning and judgment against the nations. The biblical term *goyim,* or "nations," refers to neighboring countries and to all Gentiles. The Moabites, the Ammonites, the Assyrians and Babylonians, and the Cushites all came under God's wrath during this time period.

My Sunday school class, the Basement Bible Bunch, is currently studying the Minor Prophets. As we study, we recognize familiar themes. All the prophets issued God's stern warnings to the Israelites, to the nations, or both. Like other prophets, Zephaniah offers more than God's judgment. While we find words of God's judgment against Judah and Jerusalem (1:2–2:4) and against the nations (2:5–3:8), the book closes with words of God's promise to the nations and to Judah and Jerusalem (3:9-20).

The message of all the prophets contains judgment and redemption. Words of impending doom are balanced with words of hope. God judges, and God also loves and redeems. Disaster is not forever. God's redemption offers hope. The prophets understood that God's nature is not limited to wrath.

Psalm 30, a psalm of thanksgiving, expresses the same deep knowledge of God and points to reason for hope. It says that God's anger is momentary and God's "favor is for a lifetime," a phrase that can also mean that God's delight, pleasure, or desire is life. The prophets who proclaim God's

judgment also proclaim the hope of God's redemption, and so it is with Zephaniah.

"Sing aloud, O daughter Zion; / shout, O Israel! . . . The LORD has taken away the judgments against you, / he has turned away your enemies" (Zephaniah 3:14-15). Zephaniah refers to the time when God's people would live safely in their land and surrounding nations would no longer threaten them. In Zephaniah's view, warfare against God's people was the result of God's judgment, so the end of war and judgment brought a double rejoicing. Zephaniah's insights point toward God's inconceivable grace and mercy.

Notice how all-encompassing God's mercy is. God took away the judgments against the people (verse 15) and, in effect, declared them "not guilty," even though they were guilty. God took away their punishment, which was the threat of enemies and oppressors (verses 15, 19). However, God also gathered those enemies and oppressors under the same grace.

Verse 20 promises that God will make his people great among "all the peoples [nations] of the earth" and make them a blessing to all. God will also deal with oppressors, save the lame, and gather the outcast (verse 19). This is good news to a people who are not deserving of such redemption. The mercy and grace of God are more than we can comprehend.

As we read Zephaniah, we are challenged to ask questions about our own lives. Do we love the oppressed and care for those in need? Do we allow God to heal us of our racist and sexist sentiments, of our neglect of the poor and the oppressed? God wants people to be free from the spiritual power of sin, and God is concerned with the personal and social situations that hurt and oppress people.

God rejoices when people are renewed (verse 17). Like the people of Judah, we too fall short of what God intends and desires for us. Yet, in spite of our falling short, we are the recipients of grace and mercy. We have hope in God's promises of restoration because God is in our midst and will remove disaster from us and deal with our oppressors. God's renewal in our lives as well as in the lives of the people of ancient Jerusalem is a reason to sing and shout.

How did you respond to God during a time when you felt relieved of burdens in your life? How have you experienced God's renewing power?

ALWAYS REJOICE! PHILIPPIANS 4:4-7

How are you at maintaining a calm, happy spirit? Some people are naturally that way. Not me. I tend to be a worrier in private but upbeat and ebullient with others. I suppose it is the curse of being introverted and extroverted.

"Dad, you're nervous again," says my daughter. I recognize my "worry reactions," psychologically set in childhood, and use strategies to deal with this trait. My primary strategy is to focus upon God and God's promises. Philippians 4:4-7 promises a kind of joy and peace that differs from human moods and personality traits. It promises the joy and peace of knowing God.

"Rejoice in the Lord always; again I will say, Rejoice" (Philippians 4:4). When I read this verse, I always think of a peppy little song that uses this verse as its lyrics. Does this verse mean we are supposed to act happy all the time? No, because that would be unrealistic. People experience challenging and difficult times. In such cases, acting happy is inappropriate.

As we consider the troubled economy, war and suicide bombings, scandal and dishonesty associated with people in positions of leadership, mass murder and other atrocities, and natural disasters, we know that acting happy is inappropriate. Situations such as divorce, life-threatening illness, or loss of a loved one are not occasions for expressing happiness. We know, intuitively, that the letter points to a joy that is deeper than human emotions; but what is that joy? How can we find and reclaim hope in God's promises when we endure difficult situations?

The Greek word that is translated "rejoice" means "calmly happy" or "well-off, be well, farewell" or "may things go well with you." The word was used as a greeting and a farewell and carries a wish for the good of the other. In this sense, the meaning is similar to our expression "Have a good day." The word we translate as "joy" is closely related to this cluster of meanings.

Since Paul was in prison, he may have been thinking of his mortality or of Christ's expected return (Philippians 3:20). He was worried about the people at the Philippian church, a church he loved deeply, in a personal way. He feared for their safety and survival due to the real possibility of persecution from non-Christians and to the possibility of internal conflict in the church. He desired the well-being of this community of believers.

Earlier in his letter, Paul called the church to be "in full accord" (2:2). Discord and division often emerge from bitterness and resentment, which separate us from love of God and neighbor. In such feelings we focus upon the negative and overlook the tremendous blessings of God.

A few years ago, I put on extra pounds during the week of Christmas. However, shedding the pounds took a lot longer than a week! Bitterness is like that. Once you acquire bitterness about something, you may have a hard time shedding those feelings. Finding a reason to rejoice can heal us of feelings such as discouragement, bitterness, and resentment that can take root within us. Paul wit-nessed to the deep, inner joy, the sense of well-being that comes from the grace and presence of God in Jesus Christ.

God's provision is a key theme in this passage. Verse 5 says, "The Lord is near." The phrase could mean that Jesus will imminently return, as Paul believed for his time; and it could also mean that God is near to us. We may not always feel close to God, in the sense of emotional closeness; and we may not always perceive God's provision in our lives. Many times I have not felt God's comfort at all, psychologically speaking; but in retrospect, I see the amazing ways God was working in my life during the very times I felt abandoned by God.

"Do not worry about anything," says Paul, "but in everything by prayer and supplication with thanksgiving let your requests be made known to God" (verse 6). Remember that Paul was imprisoned. He was not dispensing sunny, empty-headed advice disconnected from life's harsh realities. He was communicating his trust in God's presence and purpose in Jesus Christ. The more centered we become on God's presence, the more we give ourselves to God and become aligned with God's purposes.

Christian faith involves a growing relationship of trust in God. The result of this growing faith is an increase in our sense of hope in God's promises.

Worry is one expression of our lack of knowledge or ability in a particular circumstance. When circumstances are beyond our control, we know the power of worry. However, anxious times become an opportunity to turn to God. Our emotional feelings can be a poor barometer for our faith. "God is greater than our hearts" (1 John 3:19-20), and God helps us whatever our feelings happen to be.

Don Postema, author of *Space for God,* writes, "Prayer opens us to a closeness with God, the compassionate God we know in Jesus Christ. And the closer we get to God, the closer we get to the people of the world. . . . The deeper the prayer is, the deeper we enter into solidarity with a suffering world. . . . In prayer we assume responsibility for injustice in our self and in the world."[1] That solidarity is a result of the freedom we experience in our relationship with God.

Paul noted that "the peace of God, which surpasses all understanding, will guard your hearts and your minds in Christ Jesus" (Philippians 4:7). We tend to think of this as peace of mind, but this definition limits Paul's meaning. Peace of mind is an elusive thing, even for Christians. God's peace includes inner confidence, but it is also the quality of our relationship with God. God's peace and the ability to "rejoice in the Lord always," are the gifts of God's love and grace through Jesus Christ.

Paul gives us a model of the way we can find hope in God's promises no matter what situations exist in our daily lives. Reclaiming that hope provides the capacity to rejoice.

During Advent, how is God calling you to set worry aside and grow in joy, gratitude, and service?

FRUIT WORTHY OF REPENTANCE
LUKE 3:7-18

When I was a kid, I saw the movie *My Side of the Mountain,* about a boy who decided to live in the wilderness. The movie was loosely based on the 1959 novel by Jean Craighead George. I found sentimentally appealing the notion of living a solitary life in nature. Later, I discovered *Woodswoman* and other books by Anne LaBastille in which she tells about her adventures living alone in the Adirondacks. Both books chronicle the relationship between human beings and the wilderness.

John the Baptist lived in the wilderness of the Jordan River. During my trip to the Middle East years ago, I collected some Jordan River water in a plastic container as a souvenir. After hearing about the "mighty Jordan" in hymns, I was surprised to see how small the river is, though part of this is due to its heavy use today as a fresh-water source. Beautiful as the region is, even the stark land around the Dead Sea, John's life in the wilderness was much more than that of "nature lover." His life in the wilderness was a sign of his prophetic office.

Luke mentions details about John the Baptist that we find in other Gospels such as the description of his garments and details of his baptism of Jesus. However, we have more of John's words in Luke's Gospel: portions of his sermons and several admonitions that responded to people's questions.

We sometimes use the phrase *prophetic preaching* to mean any sermon and message that shakes people out of their routine. In the tradition of the Old Testament prophets, John warned of "wrath to come" and called the people to repentance.

John the Baptist was blunt and critical, to say the least: "You brood of vipers! Who warned you to flee from the wrath to come?" (Luke 3:7). John was a divinely-empowered prophet who fulfilled God's will by warning people of God's judgment. "Even now the ax is lying at the root of the trees; every tree therefore that does not bear good fruit is cut down and thrown into the fire" (verse 9). Isaiah used this image of the disposal of old, unproductive trees and vines (Isaiah 5:1-7; 10:33-34). John warned, "His winnowing fork is in his hand, to clear his threshing floor and to gather the wrath into his granary; but the chaff he will burn with unquenchable fire" (Luke 3:17).

We saw in our previous sessions that the prophets warned of God's refining fire. God is righteous and demands a people who are righteous.

John directly addressed the people's tendency to avoid God's demands: "Do not begin to say to yourselves, 'We have Abraham as our ancestor'; for I tell you, God is able from these stones to raise up children to Abraham" (verse 8). This is not an anti-Semitic or anti-Jewish comment. Remember that John was a descendant of Abraham and quite an important one at that (1:5). However, he warned people not to assume that their background was sufficient as a standard of righteousness, for righteousness is what we do and how God works in our lives. God's righteousness has everything to do with justice and mercy.

John told the people that instead of making excuses they should "bear fruits worthy of repentance" (3:8). What does this mean? Think of a believer as a fruit-producing plant. The plant must be healthy to produce good fruit. Repentance is a sign of a right relationship with God. Repentance means turning toward God and living according to God's will. A believer's fruit, then, are the just and merciful actions that emerge from right relationship with God.

The people asked John what they should do. John's instructions had to do with possessions, money, human need, and justice: "Whoever has two coats must share with anyone who has none; and whoever has food must do likewise" (verse 11).

According to Luke, tax collectors came to John. Tax collectors of the time had a reputation of defrauding people. Remember the story of Zacchaeus the tax collector who sought Jesus and changed his ways because of the encounter (19:1-10). John told them, "Collect no more than the amount prescribed for you (3:13). Mercenary soldiers had a reputation for taking people's money; and John said to them, "Do not extort money from anyone by threats or false accusation, and be satisfied with your wages" (verse 14).

The Old Testament prophets warned the people about unrighteousness, especially injustice and exploitation of the needy. John stood in this prophetic tradition, but his words are also interesting for what they do not say. John did not ask the people to do anything extraordinary; he called them to be righteous and just in their everyday dealings. Repentance gives people a new chance and a fresh start, and John's harsh warnings were wonderful opportunities for his listeners.

John was so compelling that some people thought he might be the messiah; but he said, "I baptize you with water; but one who is more powerful than I is coming; I am not worthy to untie the thong of his sandals. He will baptize you with the Holy Spirit and fire" (verses 16-17).

John's insight here verifies the good news, the ultimate reason for joy. God's promised Messiah is coming to empower the people. In our lives of faith, accepting the hope of God's promises through Jesus Christ, God's Messiah, gives us what we need to repent, to turn again to God, and to bear fruit in our lives.

How do you understand John's call to "bear fruits worthy of repentance"? What insights do you gain about the nature of God from John's responses to the people? How do his responses inspire you in your life of faith?

---

[1] From *The Fire of Silence and Stillness: An Anthology of Quotations for the Spiritual Journey,* edited by Paul Harris (Templegate Publishers, 1995); page 177.

Recognizing God's Promises

Scriptures for Advent: The Fourth Sunday

Micah 5:2-5
Hebrews 10:5-10
Luke 1:39-45

Christmas is inevitably a nostalgic time filled with memories of family and home. As in many small towns, the business district in my hometown is not as busy as in past years. Several stores still operate, but the large chain stores are now the major places to shop instead of the stores downtown. I remember, though, the enjoyment of shopping downtown, of seeing seasonal decorations gracing the light poles, and of braving the elements as I went from store to store. On Christmas day, we literally drove "over the river and through the woods" to Grandma's house for a family dinner.

While the season evokes good memories, it can also elicit difficult emotions. I have been blue this season because earlier this year I sold my childhood home in Illinois, ending a nearly 50-year association with that house. My father is deceased, and my mother is in a nursing home. Christmas tends to give these circumstances a sting. A friend of mine who has lost both his parents told me that a holiday movie brought him to tears because as he watched it he remembered his mother.

Our Scripture passages for this week are good reminders that we can recognize God's promises in all circumstances. Micah 5:2-5 predicts that Bethlehem would be the birthplace of one who would rule Israel. Hebrews 10:5-10 focuses on Jesus Christ as the One who said, "See God, I have come to do your will." In Luke 1:39-45, Elizabeth and Mary recognize God's promises unfolding through the pending births of their children.

When we feel at the end of our ropes, these Scriptures offer hope. They remind us that God can work in our lives just as God worked in the history of a small town, in Jesus' willingness to offer himself to God, and in the encounter between Elizabeth and Mary.

O LITTLE TOWN
MICAH 5:2-5

The Church of the Nativity is a beloved site in Bethlehem. The church, which dates from the fourth century, has withstood the difficulties of the years, including a 2002 terrorist occupation of the church. If you visit the church, you discover that the door is only four feet tall. Any person of typical height cannot just walk in but would instead have to bow to enter; thus the small door encourages reverence.

The Grotto of the Nativity is a room beneath the church and is the traditional site of Jesus' birth. It is decorated with drapery and icons surrounding a silver star on the floor. When I visited the site, someone in our tour group began to sing "Silent Night"; and soon everyone in the group followed. Is it the exact place Jesus was born? I tend to be skeptical about this location being the actual birthplace, but I was moved by visiting it.

Our Scripture from Micah honors the little town: "But you, O Bethlehem of Ephrathah, / who are one of the little clans of Judah, / from you shall come forth for me / one who is to rule in Israel" (Micah 5:2). The town was closely associated with King David. It was the home of his great-grandmother Ruth (Ruth 4:11) and his father, Jesse (1 Samuel 16:1). It was in Bethlehem that David was anointed to be king by the prophet Samuel (1 Samuel 16:4-13). Over two centuries after the time of David, the prophet foresaw the birth of the one who, like David, would rule Israel, God's covenant people.

Micah was a contemporary of Isaiah during the late 700's B.C. He prophesied during the reigns of Jotham, Ahaz, and Hezekiah (about 742 to 687 B.C.); and he was a prophet when the Assyrians conquered the northern kingdom of Samaria. Hezekiah was a righteous king who removed the idols and sacred objects associated with foreign gods. The people had a history not only of idol worship but also of injustice and exploitation of the poor.

Micah 6:8 says, "What does the LORD require of you but to do justice, and to love kindness, and to walk humbly with your God?" Micah said that the types of injustice that the Lord condemns are inaccurate scales used in trade (6:11), officials and judges who take bribes (7:3), when the powerful use their influence for evil (2:1-2), and when priests and ministers are corrupt (3:11).

The prophets taught judgment and hope, however. They taught that God holds people accountable and promises redemption. However, God's redemption is surprising and beyond expectations. Micah promised that God would make them the teachers of the nations (4:1-2). God would not only stop the current military conflicts but would eliminate war altogether (Micah 4:3; see also Isaiah 2:4).

CELEBRATE THE NEWBORN JESUS

Micah ends with the affirmation of God's clemency, "Who is a God like you, pardoning iniquity / and passing over the transgression of the remnant of your possession?" (Micah 7:18).

Micah 5:3 uses a powerful image for God's overwhelming redemption, the image of childbirth. "Therefore he shall give them up until the time / when she who is in labor has brought forth." The verse may refer to the one who will give birth to the promised ruler. It also echoes the birth imagery in 4:9-10. Childbirth is an intensely painful experience that is followed by great joy in the gift of a child. God may subject the people to judgment, but that experience is not permanent. Afterward comes the joy of God's redemption.

Not only would God save his people, but he would also give them an extraordinary ruler who would bring security and peace "in the strength of the LORD" (5:4-5). Micah uses the image of a shepherd who will "feed his flock" (verse 4). Earlier in Micah and in other Old Testament Scriptures, the image of the shepherd is associated with God as the true king (Psalm 23; Ezekiel 34; Micah 1:12; 4:6-8).

David was a shepherd when Samuel anointed him as king (1 Samuel 16:11). John 10:1-18 identifies Jesus as the good shepherd who cares for the sheep. Theodore Roosevelt said, "No man can associate with sheep and retain his self-respect."[1]

In Micah, however, the image of sheep and shepherds is more positive. Not only were shepherds a good metaphor for God, they were also an example of God's use of ordinary people and circumstances to achieve God's merciful and just purposes.

Thus, little Bethlehem becomes the focus of God's greatest promises. The monarchy did not last. In 586 B.C., Jerusalem was destroyed and the people were taken into exile in Babylonia. The exiles from the Babylonian captivity returned to the land beginning in 536 B.C.; and while they rebuilt the city and the Temple, the glory of the Davidic monarchy was not re-established. Christians recognize in Micah's words the promise of Jesus Christ, who would share David's lineage and who would reign over God's eternal realm.

In our contemporary world, we continue to experience the pain and suffering of war. We may wonder whether the promise of peace will ever be fulfilled. People of faith live inside God's promises. In this bruised and broken world in which people continue to inflict harm upon one another, we look to God's vision of who we can be and how we can live together. As Christians, we recognize that God was and is present in the birth of a Child in Bethlehem. We hold on to God's promise of a realm of justice and peace. We participate in God's promises when we live as Jesus taught us to live.

How do recognize God's promises in Micah 5:2-5? How do the promises offer you hope? Which images stand out for you? Why?

A WILLING SACRIFICE
HEBREWS 10:5-10

The promise of God's redemption through Jesus Christ resonates deeply in the repeated words of Jesus in Hebrews 10:5-10: "See, God, I have come to do your will." The Book of Hebrews views God's work of redemption through the lens of a religious tradition in which redemption and access to God depended upon animal sacrifice offered by priests on behalf of the people. Such sacrifices occurred "year after year" (verse 1) and thus stood in contrast to the willing sacrifice of Jesus Christ, who offered his body once and for all for the redemption of all.

Hebrews was most likely written in the first century A.D. We do not know definitively who wrote Hebrews. Many biblical books do not explicitly name their authors, but ancient traditions have identified those authors for us. Even the oldest church traditions, however, have no consensus as to the author of the Book of Hebrews. Suggested possibilities include Paul, Timothy, Apollos, Barnabas, and Priscilla, among others.

Whoever wrote the book was deeply concerned about this early group of believers and offered them words of encouragement and warning.

We can only speculate about the original group to whom the letter was written. The letter seems to be directed to Jewish Christians (hence the traditional designation "Hebrews") because of the many Old Testament references and emphasis on Temple rituals. The letter's recipients may have lived in Italy (13:24), and they may have lived in the 60's A.D. when persecutions against Christians involved imprisonment and confiscation of property but not necessarily bloodshed and death (10:32-34).

The New Interpreter's Bible writes about the audience as a church in crisis. The letter has a pastoral and encouraging tone that addresses several possible aspects of the crisis. The caution to "hold fast to our confession" (4:14) and the warning of punishment for those "who have spurned the Son of God, profaned the blood of the covenant by which they were sanctified, and outraged the Spirit of grace" (10:29) may indicate that the church was in danger of moving away from central teachings about Jesus Christ.

The Letter to the Hebrews became one of my favorite books of the Bible a few years ago when I wrote for *Daily Bible Studies*. Although I was familiar with the letter before, as I studied it again, the text opened up to me in new ways. What a wonderful letter! The original Greek is skillfully written and contains interesting conventions of rhetoric. The author quotes the Old Testament numerous times and discusses traditional Jewish practices. The work is like a skillful sermon; and although it has no epistolary beginning, it ends with epistolary greetings. Hebrews looks closely at God's work of redemption through Jesus Christ and calls the early church to respond in faith and love.

The letter begins with God who "has spoken to us by a Son, whom he appointed heir of all things, through whom he also created the worlds" (1:2); and it concludes with "the God of peace, who brought back from the dead our Lord Jesus, the great shepherd of the sheep, by the blood of the eternal covenant" (13:20). God's mighty work of redemption is intended to "make you complete in everything good so that you may do his will, working among us that which is pleasing in his sight, through Jesus Christ" (verse 21). Jesus is presented as the Son who is superior to the angels (1:5-14), a merciful high priest according to the order of Melchizedek (5:1-10), and the ultimate and perfect sacrifice who grants eternal redemption and access to God (9:1–10:23).

Our study contains a portion of the discussion of sacrifices. Hebrews 10:5-7 quotes Psalm 40:6-8. Hebrews 10:8-10 interprets the psalm to show how Jesus Christ abolishes the older system of sacrifices in order to establish a new way of salvation. God's law provided the Israelites a system of sac-

rifices, which are described in Leviticus 1–7. Sacrificing an animal involved the shedding of its blood because blood was considered the life-force and was believed to carry spiritual power as well. The expenditure of this life-force was a suitable "payment" to God for sin.

The author of Hebrews knew the readers would understand because sacrifice was part of their religious worldview (Chapters 9:1–10:18). Immediately preceding today's Scripture passage, Hebrews presents a basic dilemma (10:1-4). Sacrifices offered year after year in order to offer cleansing and access to God cannot "make perfect those who approach" (verse 1). If they did, "would they not have ceased being offered, since the worshipers, cleansed once for all, would no longer have any consciousness of sin?" (verse 2). Thus, Hebrews says, "It is impossible for the blood of bulls and goats to take away sins" (verse 4). In contrast to this system of sacrifice, Jesus, in his role as the perfect high priest, offered his body so that all might be "sanctified" and have access to God.

So what are we to do? In so far as our redemption is concerned, we do not have to do anything. God has already provided a new means to stay right with God. God's Son, Jesus Christ, willingly fulfilled God's will that we be sanctified and redeemed by offering his body as a "once for all" sacrifice (verse 10). God continues to hold us accountable for our sins. Instead of demanding that we sacrifice day after day, year after year, Jesus sacrificed himself and shed his blood on the cross. We are cleansed by the power of his blood, not by years of animals' blood. The promise is "once for all," but we may not sufficiently appreciate how liberating the sacrifice of Jesus is. By looking wholly to him, we know that our sins—past, present, and future—are forgiven and that we have eternal access to God.

The chapter continues with an extended "therefore" that emerges from what God has done and continues to do through Jesus. The people in this early community of faith can have confidence. They can approach God with a true heart of faith. They can hold on to their hope and provoke one another to love and good deeds (verses 19-24). We, too, can recognize God's redeeming work in Jesus Christ. We can trust and celebrate God's promise of eternal redemption through the willing sacrifice of Jesus Christ. In addition, we can gratefully offer ourselves as willing sacrifices to God.

In what ways do you see "willing sacrifices" in the daily lives of people you know? How might you offer yourself as a willing sacrifice to God's work of love in Jesus Christ in the week ahead?

ELIZABETH RECOGNIZES GOD'S BLESSINGS
LUKE 1:39-45

This beautiful story follows Gabriel's birth announcements to Zechariah (Luke 1:5-25) and to Mary (verses 26-38). It is one of a series of events in a larger narrative about God's redemptive work. Through them we learn that God is faithful and that God's promises can be trusted.

In Luke's narrative, God's Holy Spirit is active and vital throughout. Zechariah and Elizabeth's child would be filled with the Holy Spirit before his birth (verse 17). Gabriel told Mary, "The Holy Spirit will come upon you, and the power of the Most High will overshadow you; therefore the child to be born will be holy; he will be called Son of God" (verse 35). When Elizabeth's child leaped in her womb, she was filled with the Holy Spirit (verse 41). At the birth and naming of Zechariah and Elizabeth's son, Zechariah was filled with the Holy Spirit and prophesied (verse 67).

The meeting between Elizabeth and Mary brings the narratives of the births of John the Baptist and Jesus together. Mary traveled to visit Elizabeth, stayed for three months, and then returned home. The details of her visit surround Elizabeth's prophetic utterance and Mary's song of praise for God's redeeming work. Our reading features Elizabeth and her prophetic voice. Elizabeth recognized the fulfillment of God's promises in the unborn Child in Mary's womb as well as in the unborn child in her own womb.

Mary "went with haste to a Judean town in the hill country" (verse 39). Nazareth is quite a distance from the hilly region near Jerusalem, and the text does not say she traveled with others. What about Mary's parents? They are absent in the Christmas stories. It is interesting that Mary sought the company of an older relative, but her parents are not mentioned. I remember the loneliness I felt when I had no one with whom to discuss important matters. If I had known such a wise person, how helpful it would have been and how much more confident I would have been.

Matthew's Gospel says that Joseph responded favorably to Mary's pregnancy once he gained divine assurance (Matthew 1:18-21). Was the couple overwhelmed by the circumstance? Being an unwed mother, Mary was fortunate to be able to turn to Elizabeth in such a time and that she had the company and advice of an older relative.

However, rather than being an occasion for worry, the episode brims over with excitement, anticipation, and joy. Mary learned from Gabriel that Elizabeth was also pregnant (Luke 1:36). The visit gave the occasion for recognizing that God's promises and blessings were underway in both of their lives. Luke's narrative presents both women as central figures in God's work of redemption through the birth of John, who would "make ready a people prepared for the Lord" (verse 17), and through the birth of Jesus, who would be "called the Son of the Most High" and who would receive "the throne of his ancestor David" (verse 32).

In this story, Elizabeth is a prophet. When Elizabeth heard Mary's arrival, "the child leaped in her womb" and she was "filled with the Holy Spirit" (verse 41). Her prophetic words contain four key thoughts.

First, she recognized that Mary and the Child in her womb were blessed. My daughter's choir has sung beautiful versions of the "Ave Maria," which contains the Latin version of Elizabeth's words: *Benedicta tu in mulieribus et benedictus fructus ventris tui,* "Blessed are you among women, and blessed is the fruit of your womb" (verse 42). The Latin words for "blessed" used in this song are a closer translation of the Greek word *eulogeo,* which means "to speak well of." In the power of the Holy Spirit, Elizabeth "blessed," or "spoke well of," Mary and of the Child in Mary's womb.

Second, Elizabeth gave the identity of the child: "Why has this happened to me, that the mother of my Lord comes to me?" (verse 43). All the things we associate with Jesus lay in the future, yet Elizabeth recognized Mary as the blessed mother. The Child was the one the church would ultimately refer to as Lord, the respectful name for the one who is in authority.

Third, Elizabeth recognized the movement of the child in her womb as a sign from God. Her baby "leaped for joy" (verse 44). Recall that Gabriel told Zechariah that John would be filled with the Holy Spirit before his birth. We might think of this movement as a "quickening" of Elizabeth's awareness of God's work through John and ultimately through Jesus.

Finally, Elizabeth recognized the blessing of Mary's faith: "And blessed is she who believed that there would be a fulfillment of what was spoken to her by the Lord" (verse 45). The word translated here as "blessed" is different from the word used in verse 42. It is *makarios,* which means "fortunate," "well off," or "happy." Elizabeth's recognition underscores the words of Gabriel in the announcement that Mary had "found favor with God" (verse 30). Belief in God's work and promise of redemption is reason for joy.

The smallness of this story of the encounter between Elizabeth and Mary is striking, yet it communicates so much about ways that God's Holy Spirit works in every-

day lives. Here are two women in an occupied territory of the Roman Empire, yet they are primary figures in God's salvation of the world. Once again, God is not bound by our expectations. As Christians, we sometimes capitulate to the longings of the world and look for God's redeeming action in grandiose ways.

This story reminds us that God also works in small ways, in events that may seem insignificant at first glance, in individual hearts lost among the crowds, and in circumstances scarcely noticed. Elizabeth provides for all of us an excellent model for recognizing that God's promises continue to unfold in our lives through Jesus Christ. When we take time to seek God's presence, we can usually recognize ways God is at work; and recognizing God's presence is reason for hope and for celebration.

As you look back on your life, what events reveal that God was present and active? What can you learn from Elizabeth?

---

[1]From *The Rise of Theodore Roosevelt,* by Edmund Morris (Coward, McCann, and Geoghegan, Inc., 1979); page 284.

Celebrating God's Promises

Scriptures for Advent:
Christmas Day

Isaiah 52:7-10
Hebrews 1:1-12
John 1:1-14

Each year, many enjoy the beauty and symbolism of poinsettias and Easter lilies and the way they help us celebrate the seasons in which we consider life and death. All of us were born, and all of us will eventually die. We celebrate because our faith teaches us that God is with us, God sustains us, and God gives us life through Jesus Christ.

The life of Jesus, from his birth to his death and resurrection, was focused upon our salvation. Few people recognized his birth as a momentous, saving event; even fewer recognized his death as purposeful. However, Jesus' resurrection placed his whole life into perspective. His disciples understood that he was Son of God and Savior. Christmas and Easter celebrate two aspects of the same reality: God's life given through Jesus. Perhaps we should display poinsettias and Easter lilies together!

We sometimes refer to the people who only attend church on those two holidays as Christmas and Easter Christians. My father was that kind of churchgoer until, by the Spirit's power, we found a church that he loved and attended weekly. Perhaps we should all claim the title of Christmas and Easter Christians in the sense that our lives are formed, directed, and saved by the Lord Jesus born at Bethlehem, slain at Golgotha, and raised from the grave.

As we celebrate the birth of Jesus Christ and move into the Christmas season, we have a wonderful opportunity to think about ways to draw closer to the Lord during the upcoming year. Although God does the heavy work in saving and transforming us, we maintain the relationship from our side through Bible study, church fellowship, the Lord's Supper, and opportunities for service.

The Scripture passages for this study help us celebrate the boundless riches of God's presence and salvation. Isaiah 52:7-10 proclaims peace, good news, and salvation in the reign of God. Hebrews 1:1-12 proclaims Jesus as the Son who reflects God's glory, who is the exact imprint of God's being, and who sustains all things. John 1:1-14 proclaims God's entire creation came into being through Jesus Christ. Each Scripture offers joyous reasons to celebrate the newborn Jesus on Christmas Day and throughout the year.

GREAT NEWS
IS COMING
ISAIAH 52:7-10

I teach a college course on Abraham Lincoln's life. Biographers describe the anxious days and nights when Lincoln waited by the telegraph for battlefield news. No one expected the Civil War to go on for so long with such devastating casualties and destruction. When the war ended, Lincoln hugged his war secretary, Edwin Stanton, a notoriously stern person who, at that moment, was unguarded and joyful.

Our Scripture from Isaiah communicates a similar joy in the announcement of God's salvation. God is portrayed as a conquering hero returning from war. As in war, happiness comes from victory and the cessation of conflict.

Isaiah was an eighth-century-B.C. prophet who preached at the time of the Assyrian threat. Scholars believe that Chapters 40–66 of the book date from the sixth century, when the Persian Empire con-

quered the Babylonians and the emperor, Cyrus, allowed the Hebrew exiles to return to their ancestral land. The exiles had been away from the land about 50 years. Jerusalem and the Temple were destroyed. In the years following, the city and the Temple were rebuilt, as recorded in the books of Ezra and Nehemiah.

Chapter 52 portrays watchmen upon the partially destroyed walls of Jerusalem, observing the horizon for messengers bearing news. Isaiah writes, "How beautiful upon the mountains / are the feet of the messenger who announces peace" (verse 7). We could paraphrase this poetic image as "how beautiful is the arrival of the messenger" because the feet are the messenger's mode of transportation.

Imagine that you are waiting a long time for someone; and then, after your long wait, you see that person. How beautiful was the grill of my grandmother's 1949 Ford! When I was a child, I watched for her to drive down our street; and finally I glimpsed her 20-year-old car. The first sight of Grandma's car signaled the beginning of a happy family visit. Imagine waiting in a medical waiting room. You see the doctor approach, and he has a reassuring expression. The doctor seems beautiful because your loved one is all right.

The exiles experienced an even greater joy, for the messenger was simply the announcer of good news. In verse 8, the watchmen see the Lord's return to Zion. The prophet Ezekiel, who prophesied during the Babylonian exile, described a vision of the departure of the Lord's glory from the Temple in Jerusalem (Ezekiel 10). The Lord's return to Zion meant a new time and a new opportunity for the people.

Isaiah 40:9-11 predicts the Lord's arrival. How wonderful that God comes with such tenderness and concern. In today's Scripture passage, Isaiah writes that the promise is fulfilled. God has returned to the land, comforted the people, and will redeem Jerusalem (52:9). The people not only experienced comfort, but tremendous happiness. Isaiah called Jerusalem to sing: "Your sentinels lift up their voices, / together they sing for joy; / . . . Break forth together into singing, / you ruins of Jerusalem" (verses 8-9).

What a change from earlier times! In Israel's recent history, God had come in judgment and abandonment. Those days had passed. Not only would God redeem Israel from the circumstances of the sixth century B.C., but God would bring an even greater salvation. God's mighty works would be seen by the Gentiles ("the nations") as well: "The LORD has bared his holy arm / before the eyes of all the nations; / and all the ends of the earth shall see / the salvation of our God" (verse 10).

Although metaphorical, the image of God's arm effectively communicates God's power. God had accomplished great deeds of creation and destruction (48:9-10).

The Israelites had been a small, vulnerable kingdom amid great enemies; and the destruction of Jerusalem surely seemed like a denial of God's providence. However, God was faithful; and the restoration of the people in the sight of the Gentile nations vindicated their existence and proved God's power.

As we read these words, we can think of the victory of Jesus over the powers of sin and death (1 Corinthians 15:20-28). From Isaiah's standpoint, for centuries in the future God's comfort and consolation find fulfillment in Christ. At the beginning of her pregnancy, Mary sang her great hymn of praise that echoes Isaiah (Luke 1:50-53).

What a wonderful source of joy is God's salvation! We Christians are not always as joyful at Christ's victory as we could be. We become weighed down with pressures and sorrows. At church we become "bent out of shape" over trivial matters. Isaiah proclaimed joy over the peace, salvation, and reign of God and over the Lord's return to Zion. As Christians, no matter what is happening in our lives, we can reclaim this joy in Jesus Christ.

When have you experienced God's peace? God's good news? God's return to a ruined place in your life? How do Isaiah's words speak to these experiences in your life?

JESUS THE SON
HEBREWS 1:1-12

The hymn "What Child Is This" affirms the authority of Jesus: "The King of kings salvation brings, / let loving hearts enthrone him. / This, this is Christ the King, whom shepherds guard and angels sing." Christmas is a wonderful time to enthrone, or perhaps re-enthrone, Jesus as our Lord and Savior.

The Christmas season is a time when we sing angelic hymns such as "Hark! The Herald Angels Sing" and "Angels We Have Heard on High." Angels are part of popular culture. We see them as figurines sold in greeting card stores, advertising images of beautiful women with wings, in television shows (such as *Highway to Heaven, Touched by an Angel,* and *Angels in America*), and angels in movies (*It's a Wonderful Life, Michael, Dogma,* and *Angels in the Outfield*).

Some look to angels as an important part of their Christian faith, while others pay scarce attention to them. I had a church friend for whom belief in guardian angels was an important part of her sense of well-being. In the Bible, angels are messengers who often frighten people, such as the shepherds in Luke 2. They assist and minister to people (Acts 12:6-11; 27:23-25). Hebrews 1:14 states, "Are not all angels spirits in the divine service, sent to serve for the sake of those who are to inherit salvation?" *The New Interpreter's Study Bible* suggests that the concern with angels in the first two chapters of Hebrews points to the tendency of some Jews and Jewish Christians during that time to exalt angels. Hebrews is not primarily about angels, however; it is about remembering and reclaiming the identity of Jesus Christ as God's Son.

The writer of Hebrews wrote a well-organized treatise meant to be read aloud in churches, probably in Italy (13:24), that were suffering hard times and in danger of losing faith. It called the readers to remember what they were taught so they would "not drift away from it" (2:1).

Hebrews 1 makes an extended argument for Jesus' primacy as God's Son. The writer is essentially building a case for the superiority of Christ to the angels. Lovely as the images of angels are, especially during the Christmas season, the power and eternity of God is known primarily through the enthroned Son of God, Jesus.

Verses 1-4 contain a string of affirmations about Jesus. God spoke through Jesus as God spoke through the prophets (verse 1). The King James Version captures some of the beauty if not the alliteration of the original Greek of verse 1: "God, who at sundry times and divers manners spake in time past unto the fathers by the prophets." The meaning of that and the next verse is also beautiful: God has spoken many times in the past through the prophets to our forebears, and

God continues to speak through the Son.

As the Son, Jesus is "heir of all things," which also means he is heir to God's throne (verse 2). God created the worlds through him. In John 1:1-14 and Colossians 1:15-20, Jesus is the focus and meaning of God's creative and redemptive power. By knowing Jesus, we not only know salvation, but we know some of the mysteries of creation.

Jesus is the "reflection of God's glory" and "exact imprint of God's very being"(Hebrews 1:3). Jesus was a human being of indifferent means but with an extraordinary ministry; and he died a painful, ugly death. Yet this man is an "exact imprint" ("exact representation,"[1] New International Version) of God. Do you think people know you "for real"? Many of us hide our true selves from others. A person once said to me dismissively, yet sadly, "You wouldn't like me if you really knew me." God's true self is made known in Jesus. If you want to know what God is like, look at Jesus.

The affirmations continue almost too quickly to absorb the full import of their meaning. Jesus sustains all things. He made purification for sin, and he sits at God's right hand. In all this, Jesus is superior to angels.

If verses 1-4 press language in order to communicate the identity of Jesus, verses 5-12 shore up and support the affirmations about Jesus and his superiority to angels with several quotes from the Old Testament. In verse 5, the writer quotes Psalm 2:7, originally a royal psalm for a new king, and 2 Samuel 7:14, which concerns the kingly line of David. The last quote from Psalm 110:1 is repeated or alluded to several times as a key part of the argument for God's atoning work in Jesus Christ. The writer of Hebrews reveals a sense of urgency through the extended series of affirmations and the many quotes from the Old Testament. Jesus has authority as God's Son.

Although Hebrews issues stern warnings about the danger of straying from faith (Hebrews 4:12-13), the affirmations at the beginning of the book give assurance about the power and love of God revealed through Jesus Christ. The affirmations are repeated and elaborated throughout. How encouraging that we have a great high priest who is the Son of God (4:14). How wonderful to know that Jesus Christ offered himself as our perfect sacrifice so that we are right with God (9:11-14).

Christmas is an appropriate time not only to celebrate the newborn Jesus, but to think about the hope that God offers through the Son. Amid our pain and our joy, we can take great assurance in God's care and redemption. We can listen to the song that tells us "let loving hearts enthrone him."

How do you experience God's care and protection in your life? What are ways in which Jesus Christ gives you comfort and help in hard times? in good times?

"THE WORD BECAME FLESH" JOHN 1:1-14

When I was a child, I learned that Jesus was Jewish. At the time, it was merely interesting; Jesus had to be ethnically something, after all. Jesus' background was not random: The Word became Jewish flesh. The true God loved and thus entered creation through the birth of a Jewish baby. The Gospels of Matthew and Luke tell the stories of the birth. John tells us about an eternal meaning by elaborating the idea that the creative Word of God dwells with us in Jesus Christ. The ideas and images in these 14 verses articulate what the traditional church refers to as the Incarnation.

The opening of John's Gospel echoes the Creation narrative of Genesis 1 in which God "speaks" the creation into existence. God spoke words, and consequently things came into being. In Genesis, the Hebrew word has an active and challenging force; and it means much more than simply saying something. The meanings include "think," "promise," "intend," "challenge," "call," "demand," and "commune." God's act of creating through speaking engages and involves that which God creates.

The Gospel of John begins, "In the beginning was the Word, and the Word was with God, and the Word was God." This opening unifies Jesus with the creating Word and wisdom of God, and it places God's Word into a realm beyond time and space. At the same time, all things are created through God's Word, Jesus Christ.

The Greek word that is translated "word" is *logos*. It means far more than the English translation conveys, however. In addition to the act of speaking or speech, it means such things as "concept," "reason," and "ideas." It can be thought of as an ordering principle. We find the term in English as the *"-logy"* ending of fields such as biology, theology, ichthyology, and paleontology.

Ancient Greek philosophers believed that the universe was essentially orderly and rational; and the *logos* was, so to speak, God's rationality. The pilosopher Heraclitus first used the word *logos* in 600 B.C. to refer to the divine reason that coordinates a changing universe. Philo, a first-century-A.D. Jewish philosopher, merged the Greek understanding with the ancient Hebrew understanding of God's creative word and used *logos* to describe God's orderly plan for the cosmos.

In the Gospel of John, God's mighty work of Creation began beyond space and time through Jesus, God's *logos*, who was with God and who is God: "All things came into being through him, and without him not one thing came into being" (verse 3).

From this eternal realm, John shifts into a realm of life and light. In poetic terms, he claims the basic human experience of light and darkness to talk about God's work of Creation and God's truth and presence through Jesus Christ.

The first act of Creation involved light and darkness. In the darkness, God said, 'Let there be light'; and there was light" (Genesis 1:3). The image resonates in John's Gospel as well (John 1:3-4). In the tension between light and darkness, the darkness does not overcome the light.

God's Word shines light into even the deepest night. Light also illuminates. In the darkness we cannot see, but we see and understand things in the light. The Word gives life and light so that in the darkness, whatever that darkness may be, we know God as the source of life and the Creator. The darkness will not overcome us.

John tells us that God's Word came into the world, but people did not understand. Neither his people nor the world knew or understood God in the fullest (verses 11-12). John corrects any misunderstandings about John the Baptist, whom people mistook to be the light. As great as John was, he was a prophet who testified to God's light and alerted people that God's true light "was coming into the world (verse 9). What an unparalleled opportunity for those who could see (verses 12-13).

Just as John communicated to the early church, if we receive and believe that God's glory dwells with us in Jesus, we can enjoy the bless-ings and power of God. Indeed, we become children of God.

Here is the clincher: "The Word became flesh and lived among us" (verse 14). The Gospel has moved from the eternal realm of space and time into the material, time-bound world in which all creation exists. Here we have the center of our understanding of Jesus as divine and human. God took on flesh, became human, and lived among us. Some other translations use the older word *dwell* in verse 14, which alerts us to a deeper meaning of this verse. Jesus lived physically among people, but he was also the "dwelling" of God's glory. The Greek word also means "to tent" or "encamp."

One Hebrew word for "tent" is *mishkan,* or "dwelling-place." The word brings to mind the Tabernacle of the Exodus through the wilderness. The Tabernacle was a portable worship place, actually a tent, suitable for the Israelites as they journeyed through the wilderness. The construction and furnishings of the Tabernacle are extensively discussed in Exodus 25–40.

At the Tabernacle, the priests performed sacrifices and conducted worship. The ark of the covenant, containing the tablets of Law, was in the innermost room of the Tabernacle. After entry into the Promised Land, the Tabernacle moved around various towns such as Shiloh, Nob, Gibeon, and Jerusalem. David's son Solomon constructed the Temple at Jerusalem, and the Tabernacle receded into history. The Tabernacle was the place where the glory and presence of God lived and dwelled among the people.

As the Tabernacle once contained the glory of God, now the humanity of Jesus contains the grace and truth of the eternal God. Here we have reason for hope and celebration. A Baby born in Bethlehem was "the Word made flesh." The creating and ordering mind and presence of God, full of truth and grace, lives with us through Jesus Christ. We celebrate the newborn Jesus, because through his birth God came into the world.

Which teachings in this Scripture stand out for you? Why? What difference do they make in your life of faith?

---

[1] Scripture taken from the Holy Bible, NEW INTERNATIONAL VERSION®. Copyright ©1973, 1978, 1984 by International Bible Society. All rights reserved throughout the world. Used by permission of International Bible Society.